M000102627

I Can't Believe I'm
ENTRELAC KNITTING

Learn the simple secrets of this classic technique! Though it looks like basket-woven strips, entrelac knitting is actually created by making tiers of individual triangles or rectangles that you interconnect as you go. We take you step-by-step through the basic process with an E-Reader Cover. Then additional elements are introduced in a Hat, a Scarf, an Afghan, a Pillow, and a Baby Blanket.

2 13 18 24 31 36

LEISURE ARTS, INC. • Maumelle, Arkansas

Learn How To Entrelac Knit!

If you know the basics of knitting, you too can learn this intriguing technique. Follow the step-by-step instructions to make a Cover for your notebook -— digital or otherwise — while learning the ins and outs of entrelac. And, if you need extra help, you can watch all these techniques online! Soon you will be saying "I Can't Believe I'm Entrelac Knitting!"

At first glance, entrelac has the appearance of rectangles and triangles that were knit separately then sewn together. In fact, entrelac is knit in one piece with only a few stitches being worked at a time, either forming a triangle or a rectangle.

A group of entrelac rectangles and triangles is called a Tier. The Base Triangle Tier that starts this project is worked by gradually adding stitches from the cast on to form the Triangles. Other Tiers are worked by picking up stitches across the edges of a previous Tier and using basic decreases to form new rectangles and triangles.

Every Tier leans in the opposite direction of the previous Tier. In the diagram of the E-Reader Cover below, the arrows indicate the direction of the stitches as seen on the right side.

The **Base Triangle Tier** (B) has only Triangles and leans to the right.

The **First Tier** (1) has Corner Triangles and Rectangles and leans to the left.

The **Second Tier** (2) has one more Rectangle than the First Tier and no Corner Triangles. This Tier leans to the right.

The **Third** (3) and **Fifth** (5) Tiers are worked the same as the First Tier and the **Fourth Tier** (4) is worked the same as the Second Tier.

The **Top Triangle Tier** (T) completes the piece and gives it a straight edge.

DIAGRAM

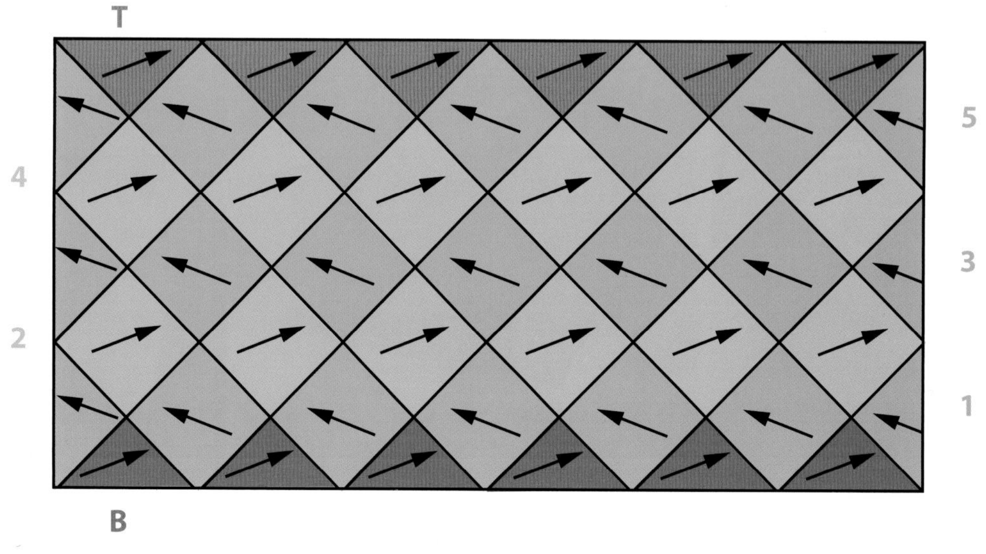

Gather the supplies you will need to make this E-Reader Cover.
We used medium weight yarn in 3 colors. Using different colors of yarn can help
you see the Tiers more easily. Don't worry if the colors peek through to
the right side as the Tiers are worked; this is just the nature of entrelac!

Finished Size:

8" x 11" (20.5 cm x 28 cm) (buttoned)

SHOPPING LIST

Yarn (Medium Weight) 🧶**4**

[3 ounces, 167 yards

(85 grams, 153 meters) per skein]:

☐ Red - 1 skein

☐ Lt Grey - 1 skein

☐ Grey - 1 skein

Knitting Needles

Straight needles,

☐ Size 9 (5.5 mm)

or size needed for gauge

Additional Supplies

☐ Markers - 5

☐ Crochet hook, size H (5 mm)

☐ Yarn needle

☐ Sewing needle

☐ Matching thread

☐ Buttons - 2

GAUGE INFORMATION

In Stockinette Stitch (purl one row, knit one row),

16 sts and 20 rows = 4" (10 cm)

If you need help with techniques used in this book, you can find clear illustrations on the pages indicated in parentheses below. Also, when you see this camera 🎥, it means that we have created free online technique videos for you to watch at www.leisurearts.com/5773. Additional help can be found in the General Instructions on page 42.

TECHNIQUES USED

🎥 Slip 1 as if to Knit *(Fig. 4, page 44)*

🎥 Slip 1 as if to Purl *(Fig. 5, page 44)*

🎥 Increase *(Figs. 6a & b, page 45)*

🎥 SSK *(Figs. 9a-c, page 45)*

🎥 P2 tog *(Fig. 10, page 46)*

🎥 Picking Up Stitches *(Figs. 11a & b, page 46)*

🎥 Crochet Stitches *(Figs. 12-14, page 47)*

INSTRUCTIONS

To begin, you will cast on and then work a series of 6 triangles called the Base Triangle Tier. In this pattern, the Triangles and Rectangles will use 8 stitches.

Base Triangle Tier

With Red, cast on 48 sts.

Each Base Triangle starts with two stitches, leaving the remainder of the cast on stitches unworked.

FIRST BASE TRIANGLE

Row 1: P2, leave the remaining sts unworked; turn.

Row 2 (Right side)**:** Slip 1 as if to **knit**, K1; turn.

The First Base Triangle's stitch count increases by one stitch on each of the remaining **wrong** side rows by working the next stitch from the cast on stitches.

Row 3: Slip 1 as if to **purl**, P2; turn: 3 sts.

Row 4: Slip 1 as if to **knit**, K2; turn.

Row 5: Slip 1 as if to **purl**, P3; turn: 4 sts.

Row 6: Slip 1 as if to **knit**, K3; turn.

Row 7: Slip 1 as if to **purl**, P4; turn: 5 sts.

Row 8: Slip 1 as if to **knit**, K4; turn.

Row 9: Slip 1 as if to **purl**, P5; turn: 6 sts.

Row 10: Slip 1 as if to **knit**, K5; turn.

Row 11: Slip 1 as if to **purl**, P6; turn: 7 sts.

Row 12: Slip 1 as if to **knit**, K6; turn.

Row 13: Slip 1 as if to **purl**, P7; do **not** turn, First Base Triangle is complete *(Fig. A)*, 🎥 place marker *(see Markers, page 43)*: 8 sts.

Fig. A

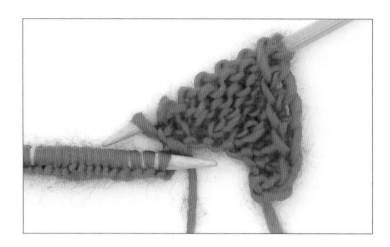

Since you are not turning your work before beginning the next Base Triangle, we recommend placing a marker on your right needle to distinguish the stitches of the previous Base Triangle from the one you are working. Remove them as you work the First Tier.

SECOND THRU FIFTH BASE TRIANGLES

Row 1: Purl the next 2 sts from the cast on, leave the remaining sts unworked; turn.

Rows 2-13: Work same as First Base Triangle: 8 sts.

SIXTH BASE TRIANGLE

Row 1: Purl the next 2 sts from the cast on, leave the remaining sts unworked; turn.

Rows 2-13: Work same as First Base Triangle; at end of Row 13, cut Red, Base Triangle Tier is complete *(Fig. B)*.

Fig. B

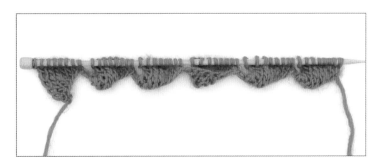

First Tier

A Corner Triangle on each end of the First Tier creates a straight outside edge. There are 5 Rectangles worked between the Corner Triangles.

RIGHT CORNER TRIANGLE

Row 1 (Right side)**:** With Lt Grey, K2, leave remaining sts unworked; turn.

Row 2: Slip 1 as if to **purl**, P1; turn.

The increase on the remaining **right** side rows adds one stitch to the Right Corner Triangle's stitch count. The Right Corner Triangle is joined to the last Base Triangle by using one stitch from each Triangle to work the SSK decrease.

Row 3: Increase, SSK; turn: 3 sts.

Row 4: Slip 1 as if to **purl**, P2; turn.

Row 5: Increase, K1, SSK; turn: 4 sts.

Row 6: Slip 1 as if to **purl**, P3; turn.

Row 7: Increase, K2, SSK; turn: 5 sts.

Row 8: Slip 1 as if to **purl**, P4; turn.

Row 9: Increase, K3, SSK; turn: 6 sts.

Row 10: Slip 1 as if to **purl**, P5; turn.

Row 11: Increase, K4, SSK; turn: 7 sts.

Row 12: Slip 1 as if to **purl**, P6; turn.

Row 13: Increase, K5, SSK; do **not** turn, Right Corner Triangle is complete *(Fig. C)*: 8 sts.

Fig. C

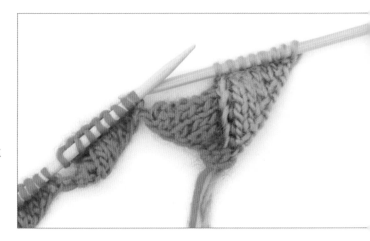

FIRST RECTANGLE

The slipped stitches of the previous tier makes it easier to pick up the stitches needed for the First Rectangle.

With **right** side facing, pick up 8 sts as if to **knit** across edge of Base Triangle just joined; turn.

Row 1: Slip 1 as if to **purl**, P7; turn.

On each **right** side row, the Rectangle is joined to the next Base Triangle by using one stitch from each to work the SSK decrease.

Row 2: Slip 1 as if to **knit**, K6, SSK; turn.

Rows 3-15: Repeat Rows 1 and 2, 6 times; then repeat Row 1 once **more**.

Row 16: Slip 1 as if to **knit**, K6, SSK; do **not** turn, First Rectangle is completed *(Fig. D)*.

Fig. D

SECOND THRU FIFTH RECTANGLES

Work same as First Rectangle.

LEFT CORNER TRIANGLE

With **right** side facing, pick up 8 sts as if to **knit** across edge of Base Triangle just joined; turn.

Row 1: P2 tog, P6; turn: 7 sts.

Row 2: Slip 1 as if to **knit**, K6; turn.

Row 3: P2 tog, P5; turn: 6 sts.

Row 4: Slip 1 as if to **knit**, K5; turn.

Row 5: P2 tog, P4; turn: 5 sts.

Row 6: Slip 1 as if to **knit**, K4; turn.

Row 7: P2 tog, P3; turn: 4 sts.

Row 8: Slip 1 as if to **knit**, K3; turn.

Row 9: P2 tog, P2; turn: 3 sts.

Row 10: Slip 1 as if to **knit**, K2; turn.

Row 11: P2 tog, P1; turn: 2 sts.

Row 12: Slip 1 as if to **knit**, K1; turn, cut Lt Grey.

Row 13: With Grey, P2 tog, the First Tier is complete *(Fig. E, First Tier shown from right side)*; do **not** turn: one st on right needle.

The stitch on the right needle will be the first stitch of the First Rectangle on the Second Tier.

Fig. E

Second Tier

There are only Rectangles on the Second Tier. The stitches are picked up as if to **purl** on the **wrong** side to start each Rectangle.

FIRST RECTANGLE

With **wrong** side facing and one st on the right needle, pick up 7 sts as if to **purl** across edge of Left Corner Triangle; turn *(Fig. F)*: 8 sts.

Fig. F

Row 1: Slip 1 as if to **knit**, K7; turn.

Each **wrong** side row will join the First Rectangle to the next Rectangle of the previous Tier by using one stitch from each to work the P2 tog decrease.

Row 2: Slip 1 as if to **purl**, P6, P2 tog; turn.

Rows 3-16: Repeat Rows 1 and 2, 7 times; at end of Row 16; do **not** turn, First Rectangle is complete *(Fig. G, First Rectangle shown from right side)*.

Fig. G

SECOND THRU FIFTH RECTANGLES

With **wrong** side facing, pick up 8 sts as if to **purl** across edge of Rectangle just joined; turn.

Row 1: Slip 1 as if to **knit**, K7; turn.

Each **wrong** side row will join the Rectangle to the next Rectangle of the previous Tier by using one stitch from each to work the P2 tog decrease.

Row 2: Slip 1 as if to **purl**, P6, P2 tog; turn.

Rows 3-16: Repeat Rows 1 and 2, 7 times; at end of Row 16; do **not** turn.

SIXTH RECTANGLE

With **wrong** side facing, pick up 8 sts as if to **purl** across edge of Rectangle just joined; turn.

Row 1: Slip 1 as if to **knit**, K7; turn.

Each **wrong** side row will join the Sixth Rectangle to the Right Corner Triangle by using one stitch from each to work the P2 tog decrease.

Row 2: Slip 1 as if to **purl**, P6, P2 tog; turn.

Rows 3-15: Repeat Rows 1 and 2, 6 times; then repeat Row 1 once **more**.

Row 16: Slip 1 as if to **purl**, P6, cut Grey; with Red, P2 tog; turn, Second Tier is complete *(Fig. H)*.

Third Tier

Work same as First Tier, joining to Rectangles of previous Tier and changing to Lt Grey in the last st of Left Corner Triangle: one st on right needle.

Fourth Tier

Work same as Second Tier, changing to Grey in last st of Sixth Rectangle.

Fifth Tier

Work same as First Tier, changing to Red in last st of Left Corner Triangle: one st on right needle.

Fig. H

Top Triangle Tier

The Top Triangles will join to the Corner Triangles and Rectangles of the Fifth Tier and will create a straight top edge.

FIRST TOP TRIANGLE

With **wrong** side facing, pick up 7 sts as if to **purl** across edge of Left Corner Triangle; turn: 8 sts.

Row 1: K8; turn.

On **wrong** side rows, the stitch count of the First Top Triangle decreases by one stitch with the first P2 tog decrease. The First Top Triangle will be joined to the next Rectangle of the Fifth Tier by using one stitch from each to work the second P2 tog decrease.

Row 2: P2 tog, P5, P2 tog; turn: 7 sts.

Row 3: K7; turn.

Row 4: P2 tog, P4, P2 tog; turn: 6 sts.

Row 5: K6; turn.

Row 6: P2 tog, P3, P2 tog; turn: 5 sts.

Row 7: K5; turn.

Row 8: P2 tog, P2, P2 tog; turn: 4 sts.

Row 9: K4; turn.

Row 10: P2 tog, P1, P2 tog; turn: 3 sts.

Row 11: K3; turn.

Row 12: P2 tog twice; turn: 2 sts.

Row 13: K2; turn.

Row 14: P2 tog using last 2 sts from First Top Triangle, then P2 tog using last 2 sts from Rectangle, pass first st on right needle over second st; do **not** turn, First Top Triangle is complete *(Fig. I)*: one st on right needle.

Fig. I

SECOND THRU FIFTH TOP TRIANGLES

With **wrong** side facing, pick up 7 sts as if to **purl** across edge of Rectangle just joined; turn: 8 sts.

Rows 1-13: Work same as First Top Triangle: 2 sts.

Row 14: P2 tog using last 2 sts from Top Triangle, then P2 tog using last 2 sts from Rectangle, pass first st on right needle over second st; do **not** turn: one st.

SIXTH TOP TRIANGLE

With **wrong** side facing, pick up 7 sts as if to **purl** across edge of Rectangle just joined; turn: 8 sts.

Rows 1-13: Work same as First Top Triangle: 2 sts.

Row 14: P2 tog using last 2 sts from Top Triangle, then P2 tog using last 2 sts from Right Corner Triangle, pass first st on right needle over second st, cut Red, leaving a long end for sewing and pull through last st.

Finishing

Using Diagram below for guidance, fold piece across center of the third Base Triangle and the third Top Triangle.

With Red, sew side seams, leaving a Flap.

FLAP EDGING

Rnd 1: With **right** side facing and using crochet hook, join Grey with slip st at seam; ch 1, work 30 sc evenly spaced across to next seam; working on Flap, work 10 sc evenly spaced across to next corner, work 2 sc in corner, work 30 sc evenly spaced across to next corner, work 2 sc in corner, work 10 sc evenly spaced across; join with slip st to first sc: 84 sc.

Begin working in rows.

Row 1: Ch 1, turn; sc in first 11 sc, ch 1, sc in next 32 sc, ch 1, sc in next 11 sc, leave remaining sts unworked: 54 sc and 2 ch-1 sps.

Row 2: Ch 1, turn; slip st in first 11 sc and in next ch-1 sp, slip st in next 6 sc, ch 3 **(button loop)**, slip st in next 20 sc, ch 3 **(button loop)**, slip st in next 6 sc and in next ch-1 sp, slip st in last 11 sc; finish off.

Sew buttons to front opposite button loops.

DIAGRAM

Sew together

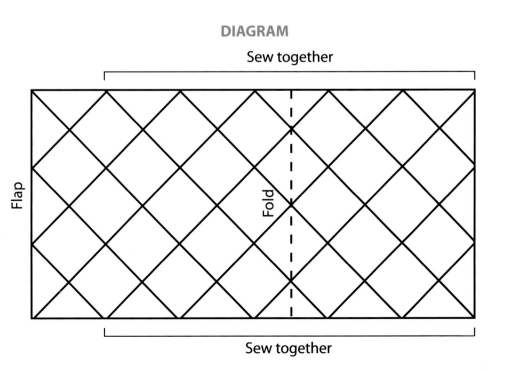

Fold

Flap

Sew together

11

Hat

If you have ever made a hat, socks, or a sweater by knitting a seamless tube, you can learn to knit entrelac in the round, too! The Tiers are here as you learned in the E-Reader Cover, just going in circles! We have used two colors so you can see each Tier. So, gather the supplies below and let's entrelac in the round!

■■■▢ INTERMEDIATE

SHOPPING LIST

Yarn (Medium Weight) [4]
[5 ounces, 256 yards
(141 grams, 234 meters)
per skein]:
☐ Green - 1 skein
[4 ounces, 204 yards
(113 grams, 187 meters)
per skein]:
☐ Variegated - 1 skein

Knitting Needles
16" (40.5 cm) Circular needle,
☐ Size 7 (4.5 mm)
   or size needed for gauge
Double pointed needles,
☐ Size 7 (4.5 mm)

Additional Supplies
☐ Markers - 2
☐ Yarn needle

SIZE INFORMATION

Size: Small/Medium
   {Large/X-Large}
Fits Head Circumference:
   19{21}"/48.5{53.5} cm

Size Note: We have printed the instructions for the sizes in different colors to make it easier for you to find:
• Size Small/Medium in Blue
• Size Large/X-Large in Pink
Instructions in Black apply to both sizes.

GAUGE INFORMATION
In Stockinette Stitch
   (purl one row, knit one row),
   20 sts and 24 rows = 4" (10 cm)
In pattern,
   2 Base Triangles = 3½" (9 cm)

TECHNIQUES USED
▪ Slip 1 as if to Knit
   (Fig. 4, page 44)
▪ Slip 1 as if to Purl
   (Fig. 5, page 44)
▪ SSK *(Figs. 9a-c, page 45)*
▪ P2 tog *(Fig. 10, page 46)*
▪ Picking Up Stitches
   (Figs. 11a & b, page 46)

Each Tier of this Hat is worked with 11{12} triangles or rectangles.

A Ribbing is worked first, providing the stitches for the **Base Triangle Tier (B)**, which leans to the left. The First Tier (**1**) leans to the right and the Second Tier (**2**) leans to the left.

The Triangles and Rectangles of the first 3 Tiers have 8 stitches each. The top shaping of the Hat is achieved by picking up fewer stitches on the remaining Tiers, making smaller Rectangles with fewer rows.

Dotted lines on the Diagram below indicates working in the round; there are no Corner Triangles, just Rectangles.

INSTRUCTIONS
Ribbing
With circular needle and Green, cast on 88{96} sts, place a marker to mark beginning of the rnd *(see Knitting in the Round and Markers, page 43)*.

Work in K1, P1 ribbing for 1" (2.5 cm).

Base Triangle Tier
FIRST BASE TRIANGLE
Row 1 (Right side)**:** K2, leave remaining sts unworked; turn.

On the remaining **right** side rows, the First Base Triangle's stitch count will increase by working the next stitch on the Ribbing.

Row 2: Slip 1 as if to **purl**, P1; turn.

Row 3: Slip 1 as if to **knit**, K2; turn: 3 sts.

Row 4: Slip 1 as if to **purl**, P2; turn.

Row 5: Slip 1 as if to **knit**, K3; turn: 4 sts.

Row 6: Slip 1 as if to **purl**, P3; turn.

Row 7: Slip 1 as if to **knit**, K4; turn: 5 sts.

Row 8: Slip 1 as if to **purl**, P4; turn.

Row 9: Slip 1 as if to **knit**, K5; turn: 6 sts.

Row 10: Slip 1 as if to **purl**, P5; turn.

Row 11: Slip 1 as if to **knit**, K6; turn: 7 sts.

DIAGRAM

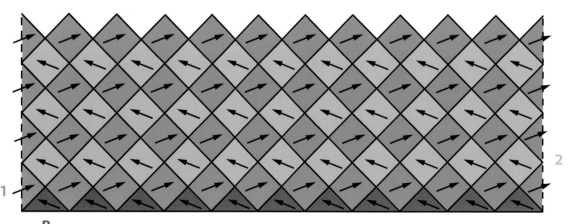

B

Row 12: Slip 1 as if to **purl**, P6; turn.

Row 13: Slip 1 as if to **knit**, K7; do **not** turn: 8 sts.

Since you are not turning your work at the beginning of the next Base Triangle, place a marker on your right needle point to distinguish the stitches of the previous Base Triangle *(Fig. A)* from the one you are now working. Use either scrap yarn or a clip style so the marker is easy to move to the beginning of the next Base Triangle.

Fig. A

NEXT 9{10} BASE TRIANGLES

Row 1: Knit the next 2 sts from the Ribbing, leave the remaining sts unworked; turn.

Rows 2-13: Work same as First Base Triangle: 8 sts.

LAST BASE TRIANGLE

Rows 1-13: Work same as First Base Triangle; at end of Row 13, cut Green, remove marker at beginning of Last Base Triangle, Base Triangle Tier is complete *(Fig. B)*.

Fig. B

First Tier
FIRST RECTANGLE

With **wrong** side of Hat facing and Variegated, pick up 8 sts as if to **purl** across edge of First Base Triangle; turn.

Row 1: Slip 1 as if to **knit**, K7; turn.

Each **wrong** side row will join the First Rectangle to the Last Base Triangle by using one stitch from each to work the P2 tog decrease.

Row 2: Slip 1 as if to **purl**, P6, P2 tog; turn.

Rows 3-16: Repeat Rows 1 and 2, 7 times; at end of Row 16, do **not** turn, First Rectangle is complete *(Fig. C)*.

Fig. C

NEXT 9{10} RECTANGLES

With **wrong** side facing, pick up 8 sts as if to **purl** across edge of Base Triangle just joined; turn.

Row 1: Slip 1 as if to **knit**, K7; turn.

Each **wrong** side row will join the Rectangle to the next Base Triangle by using one stitch from each to work the P2 tog decrease.

Row 2: Slip 1 as if to **purl**, P6, P2 tog; turn.

Rows 3-16: Repeat Rows 1 and 2, 7 times; at end of Row 16, do **not** turn.

LAST RECTANGLE

With **wrong** side facing, pick up 8 sts as if to **purl** across edge of Base Triangle just joined; turn.

Row 1: Slip 1 as if to **knit**, K7; turn.

Each **wrong** side row will join the Last Rectangle to the First Base Triangle by using one stitch from each to work the P2 tog decrease.

Row 2: Slip 1 as if to **purl**, P6, P2 tog; turn.

Rows 3-16: Repeat Rows 1 and 2, 7 times; at end of Row 16, cut Variegated, First Tier is complete *(Fig. D)*.

Fig. D

Second Tier
FIRST RECTANGLE

With **right** side facing and Green, pick up 8 sts as if to **knit** across edge of First Rectangle of previous Tier; turn.

Row 1: Slip 1 as if to **purl**, P7; turn.

Each **right** side row will join the First Rectangle to the Last Rectangle of the previous Tier by using one stitch from each to work the SSK decrease.

Row 2: Slip 1 as if to **knit**, K6, SSK; turn.

Rows 3-16: Repeat Rows 1 and 2, 7 times; at end of Row 16, do **not** turn.

NEXT 9{10} RECTANGLES

With **right** side facing, pick up 8 sts as if to **knit** across edge of Rectangle just joined; turn.

Row 1: Slip 1 as if to **purl**, P7; turn.

Each **right** side row will join the new Rectangle to the next Rectangle of the previous Tier by using one stitch from each to work the SSK decrease.

Row 2: Slip 1 as if to **knit**, K6, SSK; turn.

Rows 3-16: Repeat Rows 1 and 2, 7 times; at end of Row 16, do **not** turn.

LAST RECTANGLE

With **right** side facing, pick up 8 sts as if to **knit** across edge of Rectangle just joined; turn.

Row 1: Slip 1 as if to **purl**, P7; turn.

Each **right** side row will join the Last Rectangle to the First Rectangle of previous Tier by using one stitch from each to work the SSK decrease.

Row 2: Slip 1 as if to **knit**, K6, SSK; turn.

Rows 3-15: Repeat Rows 1 and 2, 6 times; then repeat Row 1 once **more**.

Row 16: Slip 1 as if to **knit**, K6, SSK, cut Green; Second Tier is complete.

Third Tier
FIRST RECTANGLE

With **wrong** side facing and Variegated, pick up 7 sts as if to **purl** across edge of First Rectangle of previous Tier; turn.

Row 1: Slip 1 as if to **knit**, K6; turn.

Each **wrong** side row will join the First Rectangle to the Last Rectangle of the previous Tier by using one stitch from each to work the P2 tog decrease.

Row 2: Slip 1 as if to **purl**, P5, P2 tog; turn.

Rows 3-16: Repeat Rows 1 and 2, 7 times; at end of Row 16, do **not** turn, First Rectangle is complete.

NEXT 9{10} RECTANGLES
With **wrong** side facing, pick up 7 sts as if to **purl** across edge of Rectangle just joined; turn.

Row 1: Slip 1 as if to **knit**, K6; turn.

Each **wrong** side row will join the new Rectangle to the next Rectangle of the previous Tier by using one stitch from each to work the P2 tog decrease.

Row 2: Slip 1 as if to **purl**, P5, P2 tog; turn.

Rows 3-16: Repeat Rows 1 and 2, 7 times; at end of Row 16, do **not** turn.

LAST RECTANGLE
With **wrong** side facing, pick up 7 sts as if to **purl** across edge of Rectangle just joined; turn.

Row 1: Slip 1 as if to **knit**, K6; turn.

Each **wrong** side row will join the Last Rectangle to the First Rectangle of previous Tier by using one stitch from each to work the P2 tog decrease.

Row 2: Slip 1 as if to **purl**, P5, P2 tog; turn.

Rows 3-16: Repeat Rows 1 and 2, 7 times; at end of Row 16, cut Variegated, Third Tier is complete.

Fourth - Seventh Tiers
Repeat Second and Third Tiers, picking up one **less** stitch across each Rectangle and working 2 **less** rows, as follows:
Fourth Tier - 6 sts and 14 rows
Fifth Tier - 5 sts and 12 rows
Sixth Tier - 4 sts and 10 rows
Seventh Tier - 3 sts and 8 rows

Change to double pointed needles when there are too few stitches to use a circular needle.

Eighth Tier
FIRST RECTANGLE
With **right** side facing and Green, pick up 2 sts as if to **knit** across edge of First Rectangle of Seventh Tier.

Row 1: Slip 1 as if to **purl**, P1; turn.

Row 2: Slip 1 as if to **knit**, SSK; turn.

Rows 3-5: Repeat Rows 1 and 2 once, then repeat Row 1 once **more**.

Row 6: Slip 1 as if to **knit**, SSK, pass first st on right needle over second st; do **not** turn.

NEXT 9{10} RECTANGLES
With **right** side facing, pick up 2 sts as if to **knit** across edge of Rectangle just joined.

Rows 1-6: Work same as First Rectangle.

LAST RECTANGLE
With **right** side facing, pick up 2 sts as if to **knit** across edge of Rectangle just joined.

Rows 1-5: Work same as First Rectangle.

Row 6: Slip 1 as if to **knit**, SSK, pass first st on right needle over second st; cut yarn leaving an 8" (20.5 cm) end for sewing: 11{12} sts.

Thread yarn needle with long end and 📹 slip remaining sts onto yarn needle; pull **tightly** to close and secure end.

Scarf

Let the yarn do all the color changes with this easy Scarf. Just pick a long stripe variegated yarn like the one used in our model and watch the Tiers develop!

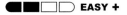 **EASY +**

Finished Size:
9" wide x 60" long (23 cm x 152.5 cm)

SHOPPING LIST

Yarn (Medium Weight)
[3.5 ounces, 151 yards
(100 grams, 138 meters) per skein]:
☐ 4 skeins

Knitting Needles
Straight needles,
☐ Size 10 (6 mm)
   or size needed for gauge

GAUGE INFORMATION
In pattern, 3 Base Triangles = 9" (23 cm)

TECHNIQUES USED
📹 Slip 1 as if to Knit (*Fig. 4, page 44*)
📹 Slip 1 as if to Purl (*Fig. 5, page 44*)
📹 Increase (*Figs. 6a & b, page 45*)
📹 SSK (*Figs. 9a-c, page 45*)
📹 P2 tog (*Fig. 10, page 46*)
📹 Picking Up Stitches (*Figs. 11a & b, page 46*)

The **Base Triangle Tier** (B) leans to the right. The **First Tier** (1) leans to the left and the **Second Tier** (2) leans to the right. The **Top Tier** (T) completes the Scarf and gives it a straight edge.

DIAGRAM

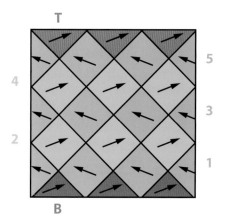

INSTRUCTIONS
Base Triangle Tier
Cast on 24 sts.

FIRST BASE TRIANGLE
Row 1: P2, leave the remaining sts unworked; turn.

Row 2 (Right side)**:** Slip 1 as if to **knit**, K1; turn.

On the remaining **wrong** side rows, the First Base Triangle's stitch count will increase by working the next stitch from the cast on stitches.

Row 3: Slip 1 as if to **purl**, P2; turn: 3 sts.

Row 4: Slip 1 as if to **knit**, K2; turn.

Row 5: Slip 1 as if to **purl**, P3; turn: 4 sts.

Row 6: Slip 1 as if to **knit**, K3; turn.

Row 7: Slip 1 as if to **purl**, P4; turn: 5 sts.

Row 8: Slip 1 as if to **knit**, K4; turn.

Row 9: Slip 1 as if to **purl**, P5; turn: 6 sts.

Row 10: Slip 1 as if to **knit**, K5; turn.

Row 11: Slip 1 as if to **purl**, P6; turn: 7 sts.

Row 12: Slip 1 as if to **knit**, K6; turn.

Row 13: Slip 1 as if to **purl**, P7; do **not** turn: 8 sts.

SECOND & THIRD BASE TRIANGLES

Row 1: Purl the next 2 sts from the cast on, leave the remaining sts unworked; turn.

Rows 2-13: Work same as First Base Triangle; at end of Row 13 of Third Base Triangle, turn: 8 sts.

First Tier
RIGHT CORNER TRIANGLE
Row 1: K2, leave remaining sts unworked; turn.

Row 2: Slip 1 as if to **purl**, P1; turn.

The increase on the remaining **right** side rows will add one stitch to the Right Corner Triangle's stitch count. The Right Corner Triangle is joined to the next Base Triangle by using one stitch from each to work the SSK decrease.

Row 3: Increase, SSK; turn: 3 sts.

Row 4: Slip 1 as if to **purl**, P2; turn.

Row 5: Increase, K1, SSK; turn: 4 sts.

Row 6: Slip 1 as if to **purl**, P3; turn.

Row 7: Increase, K2, SSK; turn: 5 sts.

Row 8: Slip 1 as if to **purl**, P4; turn.

Row 9: Increase, K3, SSK; turn: 6 sts.

Row 10: Slip 1 as if to **purl**, P5; turn.

Row 11: Increase, K4, SSK; turn: 7 sts.

Row 12: Slip 1 as if to **purl**, P6; turn.

Row 13: Increase, K5, SSK; do **not** turn: 8 sts.

FIRST & SECOND RECTANGLES
With **right** side facing, pick up 8 sts as if to **knit** across edge of Base Triangle just joined; turn.

Row 1: Slip 1 as if to **purl**, P7; turn.

The Rectangle is joined to the next Base Triangle by using one stitch from each to work the SSK decrease.

Row 2: Slip 1 as if to **knit**, K6, SSK; turn.

Rows 3-16: Repeat Rows 1 and 2, 7 times; at end of Row 16; do **not** turn.

LEFT CORNER TRIANGLE
With **right** side facing, pick up 8 sts as if to **knit** across edge of Base Triangle just joined; turn.

Row 1: P2 tog, P6; turn: 7 sts.

Row 2: Slip 1 as if to **knit**, K6; turn.

Row 3: P2 tog, P5; turn: 6 sts.

Row 4: Slip 1 as if to **knit**, K5; turn.

Row 5: P2 tog, P4; turn: 5 sts.

Row 6: Slip 1 as if to **knit**, K4; turn.

Row 7: P2 tog, P3; turn: 4 sts.

Row 8: Slip 1 as if to **knit**, K3; turn.

Row 9: P2 tog, P2; turn: 3 sts.

Row 10: Slip 1 as if to **knit**, K2; turn.

Row 11: P2 tog, P1: 2 sts; turn.

Row 12: Slip 1 as if to **knit**, K1; turn.

Row 13: P2 tog; do **not** turn: one st on right needle.

The stitch on the right needle will be the first stitch of the First Rectangle on the Second Tier.

Second Tier
FIRST RECTANGLE
With **wrong** side facing and one st on the right needle, pick up 7 sts as if to **purl** across edge of Left Corner Triangle; turn: 8 sts.

Row 1: Slip 1 as if to **knit**, K7; turn.

Each **wrong** side row will join the Rectangle to the next Rectangle of previous Tier by using one stitch from each to work the P2 tog decrease.

Row 2: Slip 1 as if to **purl**, P6, P2 tog; turn.

Rows 3-16: Repeat Rows 1 and 2, 7 times; at end of Row 16, do **not** turn.

SECOND RECTANGLE
With **wrong** side facing, pick up 8 sts as if to **purl** across edge of Rectangle just joined; turn.

Row 1: Slip 1 as if to **knit**, K7; turn.

Each **wrong** side row will join the Second Rectangle to the next Rectangle of the previous Tier by using one stitch from each to work the P2 tog decrease.

Row 2: Slip 1 as if to **purl**, P6, P2 tog; turn.

Rows 3-16: Repeat Rows 1 and 2, 7 times; at end of Row 16, do **not** turn.

THIRD RECTANGLE
With **wrong** side facing, pick up 8 sts as if to **purl** across edge of Rectangle just joined; turn.

Row 1: Slip 1 as if to **knit**, K7; turn.

Each remaining **wrong** side row will join the Third Rectangle to Right Corner Triangle by using one stitch from each to work the P2 tog decrease.

Row 2: Slip 1 as if to **purl**, P6, P2 tog; turn.

Rows 3-16: Repeat Rows 1 and 2, 7 times.

Third Tier
Work same as First Tier, joining to the Rectangles of the previous Tier.

Repeat Second and Third Tiers for pattern until Scarf measures 60" (152.5 cm) along side edge, ending by working a Third Tier.

Top Triangles
FIRST TOP TRIANGLE
With **wrong** side facing and one st on right needle, pick up 7 sts as if to **purl** across edge of Left Corner Triangle; turn: 8 sts.

Row 1: K8; turn.

On each **wrong** side row, the stitch count of the Top Triangle decreases by one stitch with the first P2 tog decrease. The Top Triangle will be joined to the next Rectangle of the previous Tier by using one stitch from each to work the second P2 tog decrease.

Row 2: P2 tog, P5, P2 tog; turn: 7 sts.

Row 3: K7; turn.

Row 4: P2 tog, P4, P2 tog; turn: 6 sts.

Row 5: K6; turn.

Row 6: P2 tog, P3, P2 tog; turn: 5 sts.

Row 7: K5; turn.

Row 8: P2 tog, P2, P2 tog; turn: 4 sts.

Row 9: K4; turn.

Row 10: P2 tog, P1, P2 tog; turn: 3 sts.

Row 11: K3; turn.

Row 12: P2 tog twice; turn: 2 sts.

Row 13: K2; turn.

Row 14: P2 tog using last 2 sts from Top Triangle, then P2 tog using last 2 sts from Rectangle, pass first st on right needle over second st; do **not** turn: one st on right needle.

SECOND TOP TRIANGLE

With **wrong** side facing, pick up 7 sts as if to **purl** across edge of Rectangle just joined: 8 sts.

Rows 1-13: Work same as First Top Triangle: 2 sts.

Row 14: P2 tog using last 2 sts from Top Triangle, then P2 tog using last 2 sts from Rectangle, pass first st on right needle over second st; do **not** turn: one st on right needle.

THIRD TOP TRIANGLE

With **wrong** side facing, pick up 7 sts as if to **purl** across edge of Rectangle just joined; turn: 8 sts.

Rows 1-13: Work same as First Top Triangle, joining to the Right Corner Triangle: 2 sts.

Row 14: P2 tog using last 2 sts from Top Triangle, then P2 tog using last 2 sts from Right Corner Triangle, pass first st on right needle over second st, cut yarn and pull through last st.

23

Afghan

There are no straight edges around this striking afghan — anywhere! The zigzag effect is easy to do in entrelac and the print yarns make it even more colorful.

⬛⬛⬛▭ **INTERMEDIATE**

Finished Size: 54" x 60"
(137 cm x 152.5 cm)

SHOPPING LIST

Yarn (Bulky Weight) 🧶 **BULKY 5**
[3.5 ounces, 109 yards
(100 grams, 100 meters)
per skein]:
☐ Dk Green - 4 skeins
☐ Lt Green - 4 skeins
☐ Red - 4 skeins
☐ Pink - 4 skeins

Knitting Needles

36" (91.5 cm) Circular needle,
☐ Size 10 (6 mm)
or size needed for gauge

GAUGE INFORMATION

In Stockinette Stitch
(purl one row, knit one row),
10 sts = 4" (10 cm)
and 20 rows = 5" (12.75 cm)

TECHNIQUES USED

🎥 E-wrap Cast On (*Fig. 3, page 44*)
🎥 Slip 1 as if to Knit (*Fig. 4, page 44*)
🎥 Slip 1 as if to Purl (*Fig. 5, page 44*)
🎥 SSK (*Figs. 9a-c, page 45*)
🎥 P2 tog (*Fig. 10, page 46*)
🎥 Picking Up Stitches
(*Figs. 11a & b, page 46*)

This pattern is made with Rectangles of 10 stitches. An e-wrap cast on is used to add on the Base Tier and the end Rectangles. The **Base Tier** (B) leans to the left and has 11 Rectangles. The **First Tier** (1) leans to the right and has 10 Rectangles. The **Second Tier** (2) leans to the left and has 11 Rectangles. The **Top Tier** (T) completes the Afghan.

INSTRUCTIONS
Base Tier
FIRST BASE RECTANGLE

With Dk Green, e-wrap cast on 10 sts.

Row 1: Purl across; turn.

Row 2 (Right side)**:** Slip 1 as if to **knit**, K9; turn.

Row 3: Slip 1 as if to **purl**, P9; turn.

Rows 4-20: Repeat Rows 2 and 3, 8 times; then repeat Row 2 once **more**; do **not** turn.

DIAGRAM

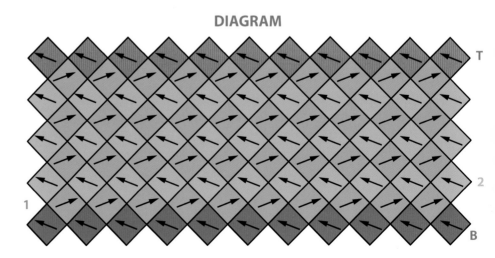

NEXT 10 BASE RECTANGLES

With **right** side facing, e-wrap cast on 10 sts.

Rows 1-20: Work same as First Base Rectangle.

At end of last Base Rectangle, bind off 10 sts in **purl**, cut Dk Green and pull through last st, Base Tier is complete *(Fig. A)*.

Fig. A

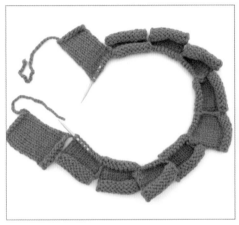

First Tier

The First Tier will have one less Rectangle than the Base Tier.

FIRST RECTANGLE

With **wrong** side facing and Lt Green, pick up 10 sts as if to **purl** across edge of last Rectangle of previous Tier; turn.

Row 1: Slip 1 as if to **knit**, K9; turn.

Each **wrong** side row will join the First Rectangle to the next Rectangle of the previous Tier by using one stitch from each to work the P2 tog decrease.

Row 2: Slip 1 as if to **purl**, P8, P2 tog; turn.

Rows 3-20: Repeat Rows 1 and 2, 9 times; at end of Row 20, do **not** turn, First Rectangle is complete (*Fig. B,* shown from right side).

Fig. B

NEXT 9 RECTANGLES
With **wrong** side facing, pick up 10 sts as if to **purl** across edge of Rectangle just joined; turn.

Row 1: Slip 1 as if to **knit**, K9; turn.

Each **wrong** side row will join the new Rectangle to the next Rectangle of the previous Tier by using one stitch from each to work the P2 tog decrease.

Row 2: Slip 1 as if to **purl**, P8, P2 tog; turn.

Rows 3-20: Repeat Rows 1 and 2, 9 times; at end of Row 20, do **not** turn.

At end of last Rectangle made, cut Lt Green, First Tier is complete.

Second Tier
The Second Tier will have one more Rectangle than the First Tier.

FIRST RECTANGLE
With **wrong** side facing and Red, place a slip knot on right hand point for first st and e-wrap cast on 9 sts; turn: 10 sts.

Each **right** side row will join the First Rectangle to the last Rectangle of the previous Tier by using one stitch from each to work the SSK decrease.

Row 1: K9, SSK; turn.

Row 2: Slip 1 as if to **purl**, P9; turn.

Row 3: Slip 1 as if to **knit**, K8, SSK; turn.

Rows 4-19: Repeat Rows 2 and 3, 8 times; at end of Row 19, do **not** turn.

NEXT 9 RECTANGLES
With **right** side facing, pick up 10 sts as if to **knit** across edge of Rectangle just joined; turn.

Row 1: Slip 1 as if to **purl**, P9; turn.

Each **right** side row will join the new Rectangle to the next Rectangle of the previous Tier by using one stitch from each to work the SSK decrease.

Row 2: Slip 1 as if to **knit**, K8, SSK; turn.

Rows 3-20: Repeat Rows 1 and 2, 9 times; at end of Row 20, do **not** turn.

LAST RECTANGLE

With **right** side facing, pick up 10 sts as if to **knit** across edge of Rectangle just joined; turn.

Row 1: Slip 1 as if to **purl**, P9; turn.

Row 2: Slip 1 as if to **knit**, K9; turn.

Rows 3-20: Repeat Rows 1 and 2, 9 times.

Bind off 10 sts in **purl**, cut Red and pull through last st, Second Tier is complete.

Third Tier
FIRST RECTANGLE

With **wrong** side facing and Pink, pick up 10 sts as if to **purl** across edge of Last Rectangle of previous Tier.

Row 1: Slip 1 as if to **knit**, K9; turn.

Each **wrong** side row will join the First Rectangle to the next Rectangle of the previous Tier by using one stitch from each to work the P2 tog decrease.

Row 2: Slip 1 as if to **purl**, P8, P2 tog; turn.

Rows 3-20: Repeat Rows 1 and 2, 9 times; at end of Row 20, do **not** turn.

NEXT 9 RECTANGLES

With **wrong** side facing, pick up 10 sts as if to **purl** across edge of Rectangle just joined; turn.

Row 1: Slip 1 as if to **knit**, K9, turn.

Each **wrong** side row will join the new Rectangle to the next Rectangle of the previous Tier by using one stitch from each to work the P2 tog decrease.

Row 2: Slip 1 as if to **purl**, P8, P2 tog; turn.

Rows 3-20: Repeat Rows 1 and 2, 9 times; at end of Row 20, do **not** turn.

At end of last Rectangle made, cut Pink, Third Tier is complete.

Fourth Tier
FIRST RECTANGLE

With **wrong** side facing and Dk Green, place a slip knot on right hand point for first st and e-wrap cast on 9 sts; turn: 10 sts.

Each **right** side row will join the First Rectangle to the last Rectangle of the previous Tier by using one stitch from each to work the SSK decrease.

Row 1: K9, SSK; turn.

Row 2: Slip 1 as if to **purl**, P9; turn.

Row 3: Slip 1 as if to **knit**, K8, SSK; turn.

Rows 4-19: Repeat Rows 2 and 3, 8 times; at end of Row 19, do **not** turn.

NEXT 9 RECTANGLES

With **right** side facing, pick up 10 sts as if to **knit** across edge of Rectangle just joined; turn.

Row 1: Slip 1 as if to **purl**, P9; turn.

Each **right** side row will join the new Rectangle to the next Rectangle of the previous Tier by using one stitch from each to work the SSK decrease.

Row 2: Slip 1 as if to **knit**, K8, SSK; turn.

Rows 3-20: Repeat Rows 1 and 2, 9 times; at end of Row 20, do **not** turn.

LAST RECTANGLE

With **right** side facing, pick up 10 sts as if to **knit** across edge of Rectangle just joined.

Row 1: Slip 1 as if to **purl**, P9; turn.

Row 2: Slip 1 as if to **knit**, K9; turn.

Rows 3-20: Repeat Rows 1 and 2, 9 times.

Bind off 10 sts in **purl**, cut Dk Green and pull through last st, Fourth Tier is complete.

Next 15 Tiers

Repeat First thru Fourth Tiers, 3 times; then repeat First thru Third Tiers once **more**.

Top Tier
FIRST RECTANGLE

With **wrong** side facing and Dk Green, place a slip knot on right hand point for first st and e-wrap cast on 9 sts; turn: 10 sts.

Each **right** side row will join the First Rectangle to the last Rectangle of previous Tier by using one stitch from each to work the SSK decrease.

Row 1: K9, SSK; turn.

Row 2: Slip 1 as if to **purl**, P9; turn.

Row 3: Slip 1 as if to **knit**, K8, SSK; turn.

Rows 4-20: Repeat Rows 2 and 3, 8 times; then repeat Row 2 once **more**.

Bind off 10 sts in **knit**: one st on right hand point. This stitch will be the first stitch on the next Rectangle.

NEXT 9 RECTANGLES

With **right** side facing and one st on right hand point, pick up 9 sts as if to **knit** across edge of Rectangle just joined; turn: 10 sts.

Row 1: Slip 1 as if to **purl**, P9; turn.

Each **right** side row will join the new Rectangle to the next Rectangle of previous Tier by using one stitch from each to work the SSK decrease.

Row 2: Slip 1 as if to **knit**, K8, SSK; turn.

Rows 3-19: Repeat Rows 1 and 2, 8 times; then repeat Row 1 once **more**.

Bind off 10 sts in **knit**: one st on right hand point. This stitch will be the first stitch on the next Rectangle.

LAST RECTANGLE

With **right** side facing and one st on right hand point, pick up 9 sts as if to **knit** across edge of Rectangle just joined; turn: 10 sts.

Row 1: Slip 1 as if to **purl**, P9.

Row 2: Slip 1 as if to **knit**, K9.

Rows 3-19: Repeat Rows 1 and 2, 8 times; then repeat Row 1 once **more**.

Bind off all sts in **knit**.

Pillow

This Pillow couldn't be eaiser! Knit in one piece in colors to match the Afghan, page 24, it works up in a flash with colorful bulky yarn.

 **EASY +**

Finished Size: 12" (30.5 cm) square

SHOPPING LIST

Yarn (Bulky Weight)
[3.5 ounces, 109 yards
(100 grams, 100 meters)
per skein]:
- ☐ Dk Green - 1 skein
- ☐ Lt Green - 30 yards
  (27.5 meters)
- ☐ Red - 30 yards (27.5 meters)
- ☐ Pink - 30 yards (27.5 meters)

Knitting Needles
Straight needles,
- ☐ Size 10 (6 mm)
  or size needed for gauge

Additional Supplies
- ☐ Yarn needle
- ☐ 12" (30.5 cm) Square
  pillow form

GAUGE INFORMATION
In Stockinette Stitch
(purl one row, knit one row),
  10 sts = 4" (10 cm)
  and 20 rows = 5" (12.75 cm)

TECHNIQUES USED
- Slip 1 as if to Knit *(Fig. 4, page 44)*
- Slip 1 as if to Purl *(Fig. 5, page 44)*
- Increase *(Figs. 6a & b, page 45)*
- K2 tog *(Fig. 7, page 45)*
- SSK *(Figs. 9a-c, page 45)*
- P2 tog *(Fig. 10, page 46)*
- Picking Up Stitches
  (Figs. 11a & b, page 46)

The **Base Triangle Tier** (B) is worked after completing the Back and leans to the left. The **First Tier** (1) leans to the right and the **Second Tier** (2) leans to the left. The **Top Tier** (T) will give the Front a straight edge.

DIAGRAM

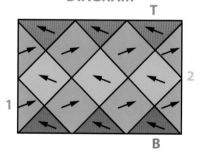

INSTRUCTIONS
Back
With Dk Green, cast on 30 sts.

Beginning with a **purl** row, work in Stockinette Stitch until piece measures approximately 12" (30.5 cm) from cast on edge, ending by working a **purl** row; do **not** bind off.

Front
BASE TRIANGLE TIER
FIRST BASE TRIANGLE

Row 1 (Right side): K2, leave remaining sts unworked; turn.

Row 2: Slip 1 as if to **purl**, P1; turn.

On remaining **right** side rows, the First Base Triangle's stitch count will increase by working the next stitch from the last row of the Back.

Row 3: Slip 1 as if to **knit**, K2; turn: 3 sts.

Row 4: Slip 1 as if to **purl**, P2; turn.

Row 5: Slip 1 as if to **knit**, K3; turn: 4 sts.

Row 6: Slip 1 as if to **purl**, P3; turn.

Row 7: Slip 1 as if to **knit**, K4; turn: 5 sts.

Row 8: Slip 1 as if to **purl**, P4; turn.

Row 9: Slip 1 as if to **knit**, K5; turn: 6 sts.

Row 10: Slip 1 as if to **purl**, P5; turn.

Row 11: Slip 1 as if to **knit**, K6; turn: 7 sts.

Row 12: Slip 1 as if to **purl**, P6; turn.

Row 13: Slip 1 as if to **knit**, K7; turn: 8 sts.

Row 14: Slip 1 as if to **purl**, P7; turn.

Row 15: Slip 1 as if to **knit**, K8; turn: 9 sts.

Row 16: Slip 1 as if to **purl**, P8; turn.

Row 17: Slip 1 as if to **knit**, K9; do **not** turn: 10 sts.

NEXT 2 BASE TRIANGLES

Rows 1-17: Work same as First Base Triangle.

At end of last Base Triangle, cut Dk Green; turn.

FIRST TIER
LEFT CORNER TRIANGLE

Each **wrong** side row will join the Left Corner Triangle to the last Base Triangle by using one stitch from each to work the P2 tog decrease.

Row 1: With Lt Green, slip 1 as if to **purl**, P2 tog; turn: 2 sts.

The increase on the **right** side rows will add one stitch to the Left Corner Triangle's stitch count.

Row 2: Slip 1 as if to **knit**, increase; turn: 3 sts.

Row 3: Slip 1 as if to **purl**, P1, P2 tog; turn.

Row 4: Slip 1 as if to **knit**, K1, increase; turn: 4 sts.

Row 5: Slip 1 as if to **purl**, P2, P2 tog; turn.

Row 6: Slip 1 as if to **knit**, K2, increase; turn: 5 sts.

Row 7: Slip 1 as if to **purl**, P3, P2 tog; turn.

Row 8: Slip 1 as if to **knit**, K3, increase; turn: 6 sts.

Row 9: Slip 1 as if to **purl**, P4, P2 tog; turn.

Row 10: Slip 1 as if to **knit**, K4, increase; turn: 7 sts.

Row 11: Slip 1 as if to **purl**, P5, P2 tog; turn.

Row 12: Slip 1 as if to **knit**, K5, increase; turn: 8 sts.

Row 13: Slip 1 as if to **purl**, P6, P2 tog; turn.

Row 14: Slip 1 as if to **knit**, K6, increase; turn: 9 sts.

Row 15: Slip 1 as if to **purl**, P7, P2 tog; turn.

Row 16: Slip 1 as if to **knit**, K7, increase; turn: 10 sts.

Row 17: Slip 1 as if to **purl**, P9, do **not** turn.

NEXT 2 RECTANGLES

With **wrong** side facing, pick up 10 sts as if to **purl** across edge of Base Triangle just joined; turn.

Row 1: Slip 1 as if to **knit**, K9; turn.

Each **wrong** side row will join the Rectangle to the next Base Triangle by using one stitch from each to work the P2 tog decrease.

Row 2: Slip 1 as if to **purl**, P8, P2 tog; turn.

Rows 3-20: Repeat Rows 1 and 2, 9 times.

RIGHT CORNER TRIANGLE

With **wrong** side facing, pick up 10 sts as if to **purl** across edge of Base Triangle just joined; turn.

Row 1: Slip 1 as if to **knit**, K9; turn.

Each **wrong** side row will decrease the Right Corner Triangle stitch count by one stitch.

Row 2: Slip 1 as if to **purl**, P7, P2 tog; turn: 9 sts.

Row 3: Slip 1 as if to **knit**, K8; turn.

Row 4: Slip 1 as if to **purl**, P6, P2 tog; turn: 8 sts.

Row 5: Slip 1 as if to **knit**, K7; turn.

Row 6: Slip 1 as if to **purl**, P5, P2 tog; turn: 7 sts.

Row 7: Slip 1 as if to **knit**, K6; turn.

Row 8: Slip 1 as if to **purl**, P4, P2 tog; turn: 6 sts.

Row 9: Slip 1 as if to **knit**, K5; turn.

Row 10: Slip 1 as if to **purl**, P3, P2 tog; turn: 5 sts.

Row 11: Slip 1 as if to **knit**, K4; turn.

Row 12: Slip 1 as if to **purl**, P2, P2 tog; turn: 4 sts.

Row 13: Slip 1 as if to **knit**, K3; turn.

Row 14: Slip 1 as if to **purl**, P1, P2 tog; turn: 3 sts.

Row 15: Slip 1 as if to **knit**, K2; turn.

Row 16: Slip 1 as if to **purl**, P2 tog; turn, cut Lt Green: 2 sts.

Row 17: With Red, K2 tog; do **not** turn: one st on right needle.

SECOND TIER
FIRST RECTANGLE

With **right** side facing, pick up 9 sts as if to **knit** across edge of Right Corner Triangle; turn: 10 sts.

Row 1: Slip 1 as if to **purl**, P9; turn.

Each **right** side row will join the new Rectangle to the next Rectangle of the previous Tier by using one stitch from each to work the SSK decrease.

Row 2: Slip 1 as if to **knit**, K8, SSK; turn.

Rows 3-20: Repeat Rows 1 and 2, 9 times; at end of Row 20, do **not** turn.

SECOND RECTANGLE

With **right** side facing, pick up 10 sts as if to **knit** across edge of Rectangle just joined.

Rows 1-20: Work same as First Rectangle.

THIRD RECTANGLE

With **right** side facing, pick up 10 sts as if to **knit** across edge of Rectangle just joined; turn.

Row 1: Slip 1 as if to **purl**, P9; turn.

Each **right** side row will join the Third Rectangle to the Left Corner Triangle of the previous tier by using one stitch from each to work the SSK decrease.

Row 2: Slip 1 as if to **knit**, K8, SSK; turn.

Rows 3-20: Repeat Rows 1 and 2, 9 times; at end of Row 20; do **not** turn.

THIRD TIER

With Pink, work same as First Tier joining to Rectangles of Second Tier and changing to Dk Green on Row 17 of Right Corner Triangle: one st on right needle.

TOP TIER

FIRST TOP TRIANGLE

With **right** side facing, pick up 9 sts as if to **knit** across edge of Right Corner Triangle; turn: 10 sts.

Row 1: Slip 1 as if to **purl**, P9; turn.

The stitch count of the First Top Triangle decreases by one stitch on **right** side rows with the K2 tog decrease. The First Top Triangle will be joined to the Rectangle of previous Tier by using one stitch from each to work the SSK decrease.

Row 2: K2 tog, K7, SSK; turn: 9 sts.

Row 3: P9; turn.

Row 4: K2 tog, K6, SSK; turn: 8 sts.

Row 5: P8; turn.

Row 6: K2 tog, K5, SSK; turn: 7 sts.

Row 7: P7; turn.

Row 8: K2 tog, K4, SSK; turn: 6 sts.

Row 9: P6; turn.

Row 10: K2 tog, K3, SSK; turn: 5 sts.

Row 11: P5; turn.

Row 12: K2 tog, K2, SSK; turn: 4 sts.

Row 13: P4; turn.

Row 14: K2 tog, K1, SSK; turn: 3 sts.

Row 15: P3; turn.

Row 16: K2 tog, SSK; turn: 2 sts.

Row 17: P2; turn.

Row 18: K2 tog using last 2 sts from First Top Triangle, then SSK using last 2 sts from last Rectangle of previous Tier, pass first st on right needle over second st, do **not** turn: one st on right needle.

SECOND TOP TRIANGLE

With **right** side facing, pick up 9 sts as if to **knit** across edge of Rectangle just joined; turn: 10 sts.

Rows 1-18: Work same as First Top Triangle: one st on right needle.

THIRD TOP TRIANGLE

With **right** side facing, pick up 9 sts as if to **knit** across edge of Rectangle just joined; turn: 10 sts.

Rows 1-17: Work same as First Top Triangle: 2 sts.

Row 18: K2 tog using last 2 sts from Third Top Triangle, then SSK using last 2 sts from Left Corner Triangle of previous Tier, pass first st on right needle over second st, cut Dk Green and pull end through last st.

With Dk Green, sew top and side seams, inserting pillow form before closing.

Baby Blanket

Soft stripes are featured in this Baby Blanket, changing colors at the end of each Tier.

The edging is a simple attached I-cord that adds the finishing touch.

◼◼◼◻ INTERMEDIATE

Finished Size: 34" x 44"
(86.5 cm x 112 cm)

SHOPPING LIST

Yarn (Medium Weight) 🧶 MEDIUM 4

[5 ounces, 256 yards
(141 grams, 234 meters)
per skein]:

☐ Blue - 3 skeins
☐ White - 2 skeins
☐ Yellow - 2 skeins
☐ Green - 2 skeins

Knitting Needles

36" (91.5 cm) Circular needle,
☐ Size 7 (4.5 mm)
  or size needed for gauge
Double pointed needles
☐ Size 7 (4.5 mm) - 2

Additional Supplies

☐ Yarn needle

GAUGE INFORMATION

In pattern,
3 Base Triangles = 5¼" (13.25 cm);
7 Tiers = 6½" (16.5 cm)

TECHNIQUES USED

🎥 Slip 1 as if to Knit (*Fig. 4, page 44*)
🎥 Slip 1 as if to Purl (*Fig. 5, page 44*)
🎥 Increase (*Figs. 6a & b, page 45*)
🎥 K2 tog tbl (*Fig. 8, page 45*)
🎥 SSK (*Figs. 9a-c, page 45*)
🎥 P2 tog (*Fig. 10, page 46*)
🎥 Picking Up Stitches
  (*Figs. 11a & b, page 46*)

The **Base Triangle Tier** (**B**) leans
to the right. The **First Tier** (**1**) leans
to the left and the **Second Tier** (**2**)
leans to the right. The **Top Tier** (**T**)
gives the Blanket a straight edge.

INSTRUCTIONS
Base Triangle Tier

With White and using circular
knitting needle, cast on 150 sts.

FIRST THRU 24ᵀᴴ TRIANGLES

Row 1: P2, leave remaining sts
unworked; turn.

Row 2 (Right side)**:** Slip 1 as if to
knit, K1; turn.

DIAGRAM

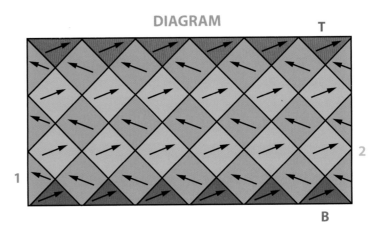

On each **wrong** side row, the Base Triangles' stitch count increases one stitch by working the next stitch from the cast on stitches.

Row 3: Slip 1 as if to **purl**, P2; turn: 3 sts.

Row 4: Slip 1 as if to **knit**, K2; turn.

Row 5: Slip 1 as if to **purl**, P3; turn: 4 sts.

Row 6: Slip 1 as if to **knit**, K3; turn.

Row 7: Slip 1 as if to **purl**, P4; turn: 5 sts.

Row 8: Slip 1 as if to **knit**, K4; turn.

Row 9: Slip 1 as if to **purl**, P5; do **not** turn: 6 sts.

25TH BASE TRIANGLE

Rows 1-8: Work same as First Base Triangle: 5 sts.

Row 9: Slip 1 as if to **purl**, P4, cut White, with Blue P1; turn: 6 sts.

First Tier
RIGHT CORNER TRIANGLE

Row 1: K2, leave remaining sts unworked; turn.

Row 2: Slip 1 as if to **purl**, P1; turn.

The increase on the remaining **right** side rows will add one stitch to the Right Corner Triangle stitch count. The Right Corner Triangle is joined to the next Base Triangle by using one stitch from each to work the SSK decrease.

Row 3: Increase, SSK; turn: 3 sts.

Row 4: Slip 1 as if to **purl**, P2; turn.

Row 5: Increase, K1, SSK; turn: 4 sts.

Row 6: Slip 1 as if to **purl**, P3; turn.

Row 7: Increase, K2, SSK; turn: 5 sts.

Row 8: Slip 1 as if to **purl**, P4; turn.

Row 9: Increase, K3, SSK; do **not** turn: 6 sts.

FIRST THRU 24th RECTANGLES

With **right** side facing, pick up 6 sts as if to **knit** across edge of Base Triangle just joined; turn.

Row 1: Slip 1 as if to **purl**, P5; turn.

Row 2: Slip 1 as if to **knit**, K4, SSK; turn.

Rows 3-12: Repeat Rows 1 and 2, 5 times; at end of Row 12, do **not** turn.

LEFT CORNER TRIANGLE

With **right** side facing, pick up 6 sts as if to **knit** across edge of last Base Triangle; turn.

Row 1: P2 tog, P4; turn: 5 sts.

Row 2: Slip 1 as if to **knit**, K4; turn.

Row 3: P2 tog, P3; turn: 4 sts.

Row 4: Slip 1 as if to **knit**, K3; turn.

Row 5: P2 tog, P2; turn: 3 sts.

Row 6: Slip 1 as if to **knit**, K2; turn.

Row 7: P2 tog, P1; turn: 2 sts.

Row 8: Slip 1 as if to **knit**, K1; turn; cut Blue.

Row 9: With Yellow, P2 tog; do **not** turn: one st on right needle.

Second Tier
FIRST RECTANGLE

With **wrong** side facing, pick up 5 sts as if to **purl** across edge of Left Corner Triangle; turn: 6 sts.

Row 1: Slip 1 as if to **knit**, K5; turn.

Row 2: Slip 1 as if to **purl**, P4, P2 tog; turn.

Rows 3-12: Repeat Rows 1 and 2, 5 times; at end of Row 12, do **not** turn.

SECOND THRU 24th RECTANGLES

With **wrong** side facing, pick up 6 sts as if to **purl** across edge of Rectangle just joined; turn.

Row 1: Slip 1 as if to **knit**, K5; turn.

Row 2: Slip 1 as if to **purl**, P4, P2 tog; turn.

Rows 3-12: Repeat Rows 1 and 2, 5 times; at end of Row 12, do **not** turn.

25th RECTANGLE

With **wrong** side facing, pick up 6 sts as if to **purl** across edge of Rectangle just joined; turn.

Rows 1-11: Work same as Second Rectangle.

Row 12: Slip 1 as if to **purl**, P4, cut Yellow, with Green P2 tog; do **not** turn.

Third Tier

Work same as First Tier, joining to Rectangles of previous Tier and changing to White in last st on Row 9 of Left Corner Triangle: one st on right needle.

Fourth Tier

Work same as Second Tier, changing to Blue in last st on 25th Rectangle.

Fifth Thru 35th Tiers

Repeat First thru Fourth Tiers, 7 times; then repeat First thru Third Tiers once **more**: one st on right needle.

Top Tier
FIRST TOP TRIANGLE

With **wrong** side facing, pick up 5 sts as if to **purl** across edge of Left Corner Triangle; turn: 6 sts.

Row 1: Slip 1 as if to **knit**, K5; turn.

Row 2: P2 tog, P3, P2 tog; turn: 5 sts.

Row 3: Slip 1 as if to **knit**, K4; turn.

Row 4: P2 tog, P2, P2 tog; turn: 4 sts.

Row 5: Slip 1 as if to **knit**, K3; turn.

Row 6: P2 tog, P1, P2 tog; turn: 3 sts.

Row 7: Slip 1 as if to **knit**, K2; turn.

Row 8: P2 tog twice; turn: 2 sts.

Row 9: Slip 1 as if to **knit**, K1; turn.

Row 10: P2 tog using last 2 sts from First Top Triangle, then P2 tog using last 2 sts from Rectangle, pass first st on right needle over second st; do **not** turn: one st on right needle.

NEXT 23 TOP TRIANGLES

With **wrong** side facing, pick up 5 sts as if to **purl** across edge of Rectangle just joined; turn: 6 sts.

Rows 1-9: Work same as First Top Triangle: 2 sts.

Row 10: P2 tog using last 2 sts from Top Triangle, then P2 tog using last 2 sts from Rectangle, pass first st on right needle over second st, do **not** turn: one st on right needle.

LAST TOP TRIANGLE

With **wrong** side facing, pick up 5 sts as if to **purl** across edge of Rectangle just joined; turn: 6 sts.

Rows 1-9: Work same as First Top Triangle: 2 sts.

Row 10: P2 tog using last 2 sts from Top Triangle, then P2 tog using last 2 sts from Right Corner Triangle, pass first st on right needle over second st; cut White and pull end through last st.

I-Cord Edging

With Blue and using double pointed needles, cast on 3 sts; with **right** side of Blanket facing, pick up one st as if to **knit** in right bottom corner: 4 sts.

Row 1: Do **not** turn; slide sts to opposite end of needle; K2, K2 tog tbl, pick up one st as if to **knit** in next st or row: 4 sts.

Repeat Row 1 around edge of Blanket.

Bind off all sts in **knit**, leaving a long end for sewing.

Thread yarn needle with long end and sew last row and cast on edge together.

General Instructions

ABBREVIATIONS

ch(s)	chain(s)
cm	centimeters
K	knit
mm	millimeters
P	purl
Rnd(s)	Round(s)
sc	single crochet(s)
SSK	slip, slip, knit
st(s)	stitch(es)
tbl	through back loop(s)
tog	together
YO	yarn over

SYMBOLS & TERMS

( ) or [ ] — work enclosed instructions **as many** times as specified by the number immediately following **or** work all enclosed instructions in the stitch or space indicated **or** contains explanatory remarks.

colon (:) — the number(s) given after a colon at the end of a row or round denote(s) the number of stitches you should have on that row or round.

KNIT TERMINOLOGY	
UNITED STATES	**INTERNATIONAL**
gauge =	tension
bind off =	cast off
yarn over (YO) =	yarn forward (yfwd) **or** yarn around needle (yrn)

KNITTING NEEDLES																		
U.S.	0	1	2	3	4	5	6	7	8	9	10	10½	11	13	15	17	19	35	50
U.K.	13	12	11	10	9	8	7	6	5	4	3	2	1	00	000	---	---	---	---
Metric - mm	2	2.25	2.75	3.25	3.5	3.75	4	4.5	5	5.5	6	6.5	8	9	10	12.75	15	19	25

■□□□ **BEGINNER**	Projects for first-time knitters using basic knit and purl stitches. Minimal shaping.
■■□□ **EASY**	Projects using basic stitches, repetitive stitch patterns, simple color changes, and simple shaping and finishing.
■■■□ **INTERMEDIATE**	Projects with a variety of stitches, such as basic cables and lace, simple intarsia, double-pointed needles and knitting in the round needle techniques, mid-level shaping and finishing.
■■■■ **EXPERIENCED**	Projects using advanced techniques and stitches, such as short rows, fair isle, more intricate intarsia, cables, lace patterns, and numerous color changes.

GAUGE

Exact gauge is **essential** for proper size. Before beginning your project, make a sample swatch in the yarn and needle specified. After completing the swatch, measure it, counting your stitches and rows carefully. If your swatch is larger or smaller than specified, **make another, changing needle size to get the correct gauge.** Keep trying until you find the size needles that will give you the specified gauge.

MARKERS

As a convenience to you, we have used markers to help distinguish the beginning of a pattern. Place markers as instructed. You may use purchased markers or tie a length of contrasting color yarn around the needle. Remove the marker(s) as instructed or when no longer needed.

KNITTING IN THE ROUND USING CIRCULAR NEEDLES

When you knit the ribbing for the Hat, page 12, you are going to work around on the outside of a circle with the **right** side of the knitting facing you throughout the Ribbing.

Using a circular needle, cast on all stitches as instructed. Untwist and straighten the stitches on the needle to be sure that the cast on ridge lies on the inside of the needle and never rolls around the needle.

Hold the needle so that the working yarn is attached to the stitch closest to the right hand point. Place a marker to mark the beginning of the round.
To begin working in the round, work the stitches on the left hand point *(Fig. 1)*.

After checking that the cast on edge has not twisted around the needle, continue working each round as instructed without turning the work **until** you are instructed to do so while working the Base Triangle Tier.

Fig. 1

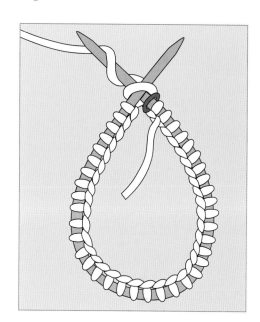

Yarn Weight Symbol & Names	LACE ⓪	SUPER FINE ①	FINE ②	LIGHT ③	MEDIUM ④	BULKY ⑤	SUPER BULKY ⑥
Type of Yarns in Category	Fingering, size 10 crochet thread	Sock, Fingering, Baby	Sport, Baby	DK, Light Worsted	Worsted, Afghan, Aran	Chunky, Craft, Rug	Bulky, Roving
Knit Gauge Range* in Stockinette St to 4" (10 cm)	33-40** sts	27-32 sts	23-26 sts	21-24 sts	16-20 sts	12-15 sts	6-11 sts
Advised Needle Size Range	000-1	1 to 3	3 to 5	5 to 7	7 to 9	9 to 11	11 and larger

*GUIDELINES ONLY: The chart above reflects the most commonly used gauges and needle sizes for specific yarn categories.

** Lace weight yarns are usually knitted on larger needles to create lacy openwork patterns. Accordingly, a gauge range is difficult to determine. Always follow the gauge stated in your pattern.

USING DOUBLE POINTED KNITTING NEEDLES

When working a piece that is too small to use a circular needle, double pointed needles are required. Divide the stitches into thirds and slip one-third of the stitches onto each of 3 double pointed needles, forming a triangle. With the fourth needle, work across the stitches on the first needle (*Fig. 2*).

Fig. 2

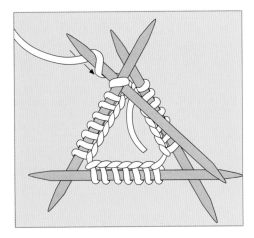

E-WRAP CAST ON

Make a backward loop with the working yarn and place on right hand needle (*Fig. 3*).

Fig. 3

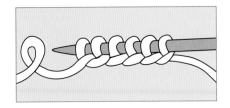

SLIP 1 AS IF TO KNIT

When instructed to slip 1 as if to **knit**, with yarn in back, insert the right needle from **left** to **right** in the stitch on the left needle (*Fig. 4*) and slip it to the right needle.

Fig. 4

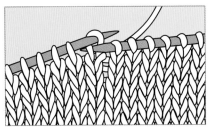

SLIP 1 AS IF TO PURL

When instructed to slip 1 as if to **purl**, with yarn in back, insert the right needle from **right** to **left** in the stitch on the left needle (*Fig. 5*) and slip it to the right needle.

Fig. 5

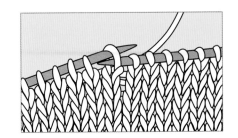

INCREASE

Knit the next stitch but do **not** slip the old stitch off the left needle (*Fig. 6a*). Insert the right needle into the back loop of the same stitch and **knit** it (*Fig. 6b*), then slip the old stitch off the left needle.

Fig. 6a

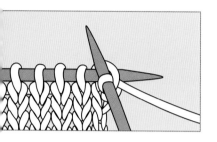

Fig. 6b

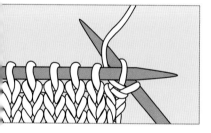

DECREASES
KNIT 2 TOGETHER

(*abbreviated K2 tog*)

Insert the right needle into the **front** of the first two stitches on the left needle as if to **knit** (*Fig. 7*), then **knit** them together as if they were one stitch.

Fig. 7

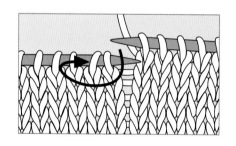

KNIT 2 TOGETHER THROUGH THE BACK LOOP

(*abbreviated K2 tog tbl*)

Insert the right needle into the **back** of the first two stitches on the left needle (*Fig. 8*), then knit them together as if they were one stitch.

Fig. 8

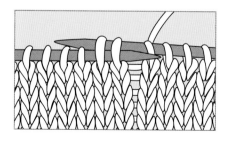

SLIP, SLIP, KNIT

(*abbreviated SSK*)

Separately slip two stitches as if to **knit** (*Fig. 9a*). Insert the left needle into the **front** of both slipped stitches (*Fig. 9b*) and **knit** them together as if they were one stitch (*Fig. 9c*).

Fig. 9a

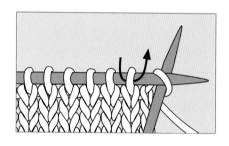

Fig. 9b

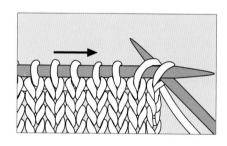

Fig. 9c

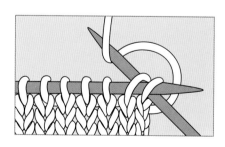

PURL 2 TOGETHER

(abbreviated P2 tog)

Insert the right needle into the **front** of the first two stitches on the left needle as if to **purl** *(Fig. 10)*, then purl them together as if they were one stitch.

Fig. 10

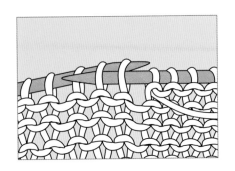

PICKING UP STITCHES

When instructed to pick up stitches as if to **knit**, with the **right** side facing, insert the needle from the **front** to the **back** under two strands at the edge of the worked piece *(Fig. 11a)*. Put the yarn around the needle as if to **knit**, then bring the needle with the yarn back through the stitch to the right side, resulting in a stitch on the needle.

Repeat this across the edge, picking up the required number of stitches. A crochet hook may be helpful to pull the yarn through.

Fig. 11a

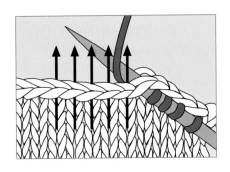

When instructed to pick up stitches as if to **purl**, with the **wrong** side facing, insert the needle from the **back** to the **front** under two strands at the edge of the worked piece *(Fig. 11b)*. Put the yarn around the needle as if to **purl**, then bring the needle with the yarn back through the stitch to the right side, resulting in a stitch on the needle.

Repeat this across the edge, picking up the required number of stitches. A crochet hook may be helpful to pull the yarn through.

Fig. 11b

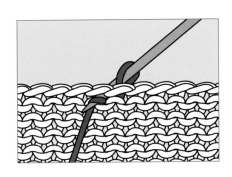

CROCHET STITCHES

CHAIN (abbreviated ch)

Begin with a slip knot on the hook. Bring the yarn **over** the hook from back to front, catching the yarn with the hook and turning the hook slightly towards you to keep the yarn from slipping off. Draw the yarn through the slip knot (*Fig. 12*) (**first chain st made**).

Fig. 12

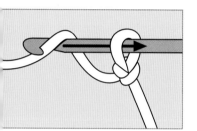

SLIP STITCH (abbreviated slip st)

Insert hook in stitch indicated, YO and draw through stitch and loop on hook (*Fig. 13*) (**slip stitch made**).

Fig. 13

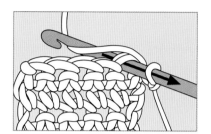

SINGLE CROCHET

(abbreviated sc)

Insert hook in stitch indicated, YO and pull up a loop (2 loops on hook), YO and draw through both loops on hook (*Fig. 14*) (**single crochet made**).

Fig. 14

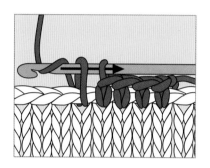

Meet the Designer

Marlaina "Marly" Bird is a bi-craftsy girl who both knits and crochets. Having grown up watching her grandmother crochet, she finally convinced her grandmother to teach her how in 1999. From that point on, she was hooked.

"Crochet became a part of my life," she said. "I didn't go anywhere without my yarn and a hook." Within two years, she was creating her own designs. After a friend taught her to knit in 2004, Marly was equally addicted. Her passion for working with yarn soon led Marly to leave her job in financial services and launch her Yarn Thing podcast, where yarn is the star and there is no rivalry between knitting and crochet.

A wife and the mother of three kids, Marly is creative director for Bijou Basin Ranch Yarns luxury yak fiber and teaches knitting and crochet workshops around the country and on Craftsy.com. She is co-author of the Leisure Arts book, *Curvy Crochet*, and her designs have been published in numerous magazines and books.

For more about Marly, visit her website at marlybird.com and listen to her podcast at blogtalkradio.com/yarnthing.

Yarn Information

Projects in this book were made using a variety of yarn weights. Any brand of the specified weight of yarn may be used. It is best to refer to the yardage/meters when determining how many balls or skeins to purchase. Remember, to arrive at the finished size, it is the GAUGE/TENSION that is important, not the brand of yarn.

For your convenience, listed below are the specific yarns used to create our photography models.

E-READER COVER
Caron® Vickie Howell Sheep(ish)
Red - #0015 Red(ish)
Lt Grey - #0003 Grey(ish)
Grey - #0002 Gun Metal(ish)

HAT
Red Heart® Soft
Green - #9523 Dark Leaf
Variegated - #9938 Goulash

SCARF
Red Heart® Boutique® Treasure™
#1913 Spectrum

AFGHAN
Premier® Yarns Debra Norville
Serenity® Chunky Prints
Dk Green - #6003 Forest
Lt Green - #5010 Apple Orchard
Red - #6002 Red Bayou
Pink - #0044 Berry Burst

PILLOW
Premier® Yarns Debra Norville
Serenity® Chunky Prints
Dk Green - #6003 Forest
Lt Green - #5010 Apple Orchard
Red - #6002 Red Bayou
Pink - #0044 Berry Burst

BABY BLANKET
Red Heart® Soft Baby Steps™
Blue - #9800 Baby Blue
White - #9600 White
Yellow - #9200 Baby Yellow
Green - #9620 Baby Green

We have made every effort to ensure that these instructions are accurate and complete. We cannot, however, be responsible for human error, typographical mistakes, or variations in individual work.

Production Team: Writer/Instructional Editor - Sarah J. Green; Editorial Writer - Susan Frantz Wiles; Graphic Artist - Becca Snider Tally; Senior Graphic Artist - Lora Puls; Photo Stylist - Lori Wenger; and Photographers - Mark Mathews and Ken West.

Items made and instructions tested by Raymelle Greening.